I0017035

50+ LINUX COMMANDS

before joining a Company

DCI series

4th Edition

Aditya Chatterjee x Benjamin QoChuk

 OPENGENUS

BE A NATIONAL PROGRAMMER

INTRODUCTION

This book will change your UNIX development skills forever. Read it now to level up your future.

Best way to master LINUX COMMANDS in 2 hours. Includes Linux Command CHEATSHEET (goldmine).

Linux and its variants like Ubuntu, RedHat, OpenSUSE and others are the preferred development workspace for most serious developers today.

For interviews, it is important to have an idea of basic Linux commands as not being comfortable in using Linux will be a red flag in Coding Interviews.

This book "**50+ Linux Commands before joining a Company**" will prepare you to use Linux in a way a professional developer would use. You can fit in any developer group instantly and will feel confident in using your UNIX computing system.

The first chapter is the LINUX COMMANDS cheatsheet. This is a **goldmine**. This will help you get the core idea of over 50 important Linux commands within 30 minutes. You should revisit and revise this cheatsheet every 2 months.

In the following chapters, we have covered **over 50 commands in depth with examples and explanation**, and this will enable you to use Linux efficiently for any basic development work. All commands are important and has been chosen by analyzing the development work done in top companies.

High level ideas we have covered are:

- Get hardware details about your system
- Get software details about your system
- Running and handling processes efficiently and in background
- Handling file system
- Other key commands

At the end, we have present **key advices of using Linux** that will make you a *"great developer"* clearly.

Let us get started directly by capturing the details of the current computing system.

This is important so that you can share the details along with the main work (may be an application or benchmark data) so it is reproducible.

This book is for:

- Students preparing for Coding Interviews.
- Developers who plan to work in a company as a developer.
- Developers joining their first full-time job or internship in few days and want to make the best first impression.

Get started with this book and change the equation of your career.

Book: **50+ Linux Commands before joining a Company**

Authors (2): Aditya Chatterjee, Benjamin QoChuk

About the authors:

Aditya Chatterjee is an Independent Researcher, Technical Author and the Founding Member of OPENGENUS, a scientific community focused on Computing Technology.

Benjamin QoChuk is a Computer Science Researcher, Inventor and Software Developer. He has worked several companies across USA and Japan and is currently, an Academic Researcher at OPENGENUS.His educational background include Bachelors at Vanderbilt University and PhD in Computer Science at Peking University.

Published: August 2020 (Edition 1)

Updated: September 2024 (Edition 4)

Pages: 71

Publisher: © OpenGenus

ISBN: 9798673093863

Contact us: team@opengenus.org

Available on Amazon as Paperback and Hardcover exclusively.

TABLE OF CONTENTS

RECOMMENDED BOOKS

DAILY43: Best way to master EASY tagged Coding problems in a month with to-the-point explanation.

No need to practice 1000s of problems over years. This book covers all coding patterns.

Get **DAILY43** on Amazon: **amzn.to/4cVoEdK**

Series you should read:

- Day before Coding Interview [DCI] series: **amzn.to/3XAH8f9**
- Coding Interview DSA series: **amzn.to/3z7NbOQ**

CHEATSHEET: Linux Commands

Following table summarizes the important Linux commands that you should know how to use (explained with sample commands):

Command	Sample Usage	Description
ls	ls	Lists files and directories in the current directory.
	ls -l	Lists files and directories in the current directory with detailed information.
	ls -a	Lists all files, including hidden files (those starting with a dot).
cd	cd /home/user	Changes the current directory to /home/user.
	cd ..	Moves up one directory level (parent directory).
pwd	pwd	Prints the current working directory path.
cp	cp file.txt /backup/	Copies file.txt to the /backup/ directory.
	cp -r /srcdir /dstdir	Recursively copies the /srcdir directory to /dstdir.
mv	mv file.txt /newfolder/	Moves file.txt to /newfolder/.
	mv oldname.txt newname.txt	Renames oldname.txt to newname.txt.

rm	rm file.txt	Deletes file.txt.
	rm -rf /directoryName	Deletes a directory and its contents recursively.
touch	touch newfile.txt	Creates an empty file named newfile.txt.
vi	vi text.txt	Open the file text.txt using vi editor
After entering the file	Press I key	To edit the file
Press ESC key (after entering the file)	Type :25	To go to line number 25
	Type :set nu	Enables line numbers
	Type :set nonu	Disable line numbers
	Type /word (then ENTER)	To search "word" in the file
	After above command, press the key N	To go to the next occurrence of "word"
	After above command, press the key SHIFT + N	To go to the previous occurrence of "word"
	Type :wq (then ENTER key)	To save changes and close file
	Type :q! (then ENTER key)	To close file without saving the changes.
	Type dd	To delete current line
	Type 7dd	To delete the next 7 lines

	Press SHIFT + G	To go to the end of the file
grep	grep "word" file.txt	Searches for "word" in file.txt.
	grep -ir "word" /directory	Recursively searches for "word" in /directory, case-insensitively.
find	find / -name file.txt	Searches for file.txt starting from the root directory.
	find . -type f -name "*.txt"	Finds all .txt files in the current directory and subdirectories.
mkdir	mkdir newdir	Creates a new directory named newdir.
	mkdir -p /parentdir/newdir	Creates a directory tree, including parent directories if they do not exist.
rmdir	rmdir olddir	Removes an empty directory named olddir.
	rmdir -p /parentdir/newdir	Removes a directory tree, only if empty.
cat	cat file.txt	Displays the contents of file.txt.
	cat file1.txt file2.txt > merged.txt	Concatenates file1.txt and file2.txt into merged.txt.
echo	echo "Hello"	Prints "Hello" to the terminal or a file.
	echo "Hello" >> file.txt	Appends "Hello" to file.txt.
chmod	chmod 755 script.sh	Changes permissions of script.sh to 755 (rwxr-xr-x).
	chmod +x script.sh	Makes script.sh executable.

nohup	nohup command &	To run the "command" in background even when the session is closed.
chown	chown user:user file.txt	Changes the owner and group of file.txt.
	chown -R user:user /directory	Recursively changes the owner and group of /directory.
cron	* * * * * command	Syntax: Minute (0 to 59) Hour (0 - 23) Day (1 to 31) Month (1 - 12) Day of week (0 to 7) command
	* * * * * ./script.sh	Runs script.sh every minute
	30 2 * * 1 ./script.sh	Runs script.sh every Monday at 2:30 AM
	0 22 * * 1-5 ./script.sh	Runs script.sh at 10:00 PM, Monday to Friday
tar	tar -czvf archive.tar.gz /dir	Compresses /dir into a .tar.gz archive.
	tar -xzvf archive.tar.gz	Extracts the contents of archive.tar.gz.
df	df -h	Displays disk space usage in a human-readable format.
	df -Th	Displays disk space usage with filesystem type.
du	du -sh /dir	Displays the size of /dir and its contents.
	du -ah /dir	Displays the size of all files and directories within /dir.
ps	ps aux	Displays a list of running processes.
	ps -ef	Displays detailed information about all running processes.

kill	kill 1234	Terminates the process with PID 1234.
	kill -9 1234	Forcibly terminates the process with PID 1234.
top	top	Displays real-time system resource usage.
htop	htop	Interactive process viewer with more visual information than top.
man	man ls	Displays the manual for the ls command.
	man -k keyword	Searches the manual pages for a keyword.
ssh	ssh user@hostname	Connects to a remote host via SSH.
	ssh -i keyfile.pem user@hostname	Connects to a remote host via SSH using a private key.
scp	scp file.txt user@remote:/path	Securely copies file.txt to a remote host.
	scp -r /dir user@remote:/path	Securely copies a directory recursively to a remote host.
sudo	sudo apt-get update	Runs the apt-get update command with superuser privileges.
	sudo reboot	Reboots the system.
apt-get	sudo apt-get install package	Installs package on a Debian-based system.
	sudo apt-get remove package	Removes package from a Debian-based system.
yum	sudo yum install package	Installs package on a Red Hat-based system.

	sudo yum update	Updates all installed packages on a Red Hat-based system.
service	sudo service apache2 start	Starts the Apache service.
	sudo service apache2 restart	Restarts the Apache service.
systemct l	sudo systemctl start nginx	Starts the NGINX service.
	sudo systemctl enable nginx	Enables the NGINX service to start at boot.
ifconfig	ifconfig	Displays or configures network interfaces.
	ifconfig eth0 up	Brings the eth0 interface up.
ip	ip addr show	Displays IP addresses and property information of network interfaces.
	ip link set eth0 up	Brings the eth0 interface up.
ping	ping google.com	Sends ICMP echo requests to test network connectivity.
	ping -c 4 google.com	Sends 4 ICMP echo requests to google.com.
wget	wget https://example.com/file.zip	Downloads file.zip from example.com.
curl	curl -O https://example.com/file.zip	Downloads file.zip from example.com using curl.
	curl -I https://example.com	Fetches HTTP headers from example.com.
netstat	netstat -tuln	Displays listening ports and services.

ss	ss -tuln	Displays socket statistics, including listening ports.
mount	mount /dev/sda1 /mnt	Mounts the /dev/sda1 partition to /mnt.
umount	umount /mnt	Unmounts the partition mounted at /mnt.
df	df -h	Displays disk space usage in human-readable format.
free	free -m	Displays memory usage in megabytes.
uname	uname -a	Displays detailed system information.
hostname	hostname	Displays or sets the system's hostname.
history	history	Displays the command history.
alias	alias ll='ls -la'	Creates an alias ll for the ls -la command.
unalias	unalias ll	Removes the ll alias.
export	export PATH=$PATH:/new/path	Adds /new/path to the PATH environment variable.
unset	unset PATH	Removes the environment variable PATH.
env	env	Displays the current environment variables.
date	date	Displays the current date and time.
cal	cal	Displays the current month's calendar.

reboot	sudo reboot	Reboots the system.
shutdown	sudo shutdown -h now	Shuts down the system immediately.
uptime	uptime	Displays the system uptime.
who	who	Displays who is logged into the system.
uname	uname -r	Displays the kernel version.
locate	locate file.txt	Quickly finds the location of file.txt.
updatedb	sudo updatedb	Updates the database used by locate.
basename	basename /path/to/file.txt	Strips the directory path and returns the filename.
dirname	dirname /path/to/file.txt	Strips the filename and returns the directory path.

KEY POINTS

Following are key points regarding Linux operating system in short:

- **Everything is a File**: In Linux, almost everything is treated as a file, including hardware devices, directories, and processes. This uniformity simplifies the interaction with system resources.
- **File System Hierarchy**: Linux uses a **hierarchical directory structure**, with the root directory (/) at the top. All files and directories start from this root.

- **Root User**: The root user is the superuser with unrestricted access to all commands and files in the system. It is used for administrative tasks.

- **Permissions**: Linux uses permissions system to control who can read, write, or execute a file. Permissions are set for three categories: the owner, the group, and others.

- **Processes**: A process is an instance of a running program. Linux allows multiple processes to run simultaneously, and each process is assigned a **unique process ID (PID)**.

- **Daemons**: Daemons are background processes that start during boot and run continuously to handle system or service requests, like **cron** (for scheduling tasks) and **sshd** (for SSH connections).

- **Shell**: The shell is a command-line interface that allows users to interact with the operating system by executing commands. Bash (Bourne Again Shell) is the most common shell in Linux.

- **Package Management**: Linux uses package managers like apt, yum, or dnf to install, update, and manage software packages. These tools simplify software management on the system.

- **Kernel**: The kernel is the core part of the Linux operating system, managing hardware resources and providing essential services to applications.

- **Init System**: The init system is responsible for booting the system and managing services. Common init systems include systemd, SysVinit, and Upstart.

- **Terminal/Console**: The terminal is a text-based interface that allows users to input commands directly to the operating system. It's a powerful tool for system administration.

- **File Types**: Linux recognizes several file types, including regular files, directories, symbolic links, character devices, and block devices.

- **Mounting**: Mounting is the process of making a filesystem accessible at a certain point in the directory tree. This is how storage devices and filesystems are integrated into the Linux directory structure.
- **Swap Space**: Swap is a special area on the disk used when the system runs out of RAM. It temporarily holds data that's not actively being used, helping to manage memory.
- **Symlinks and Hard Links**: A symbolic link (symlink) is a file that points to another file or directory, while a hard link is an additional name for an existing file.
- **Pipes and Redirection**: Pipes (|) allow the output of one command to be used as the input to another. Redirection (>, >>, <) is used to redirect output to files or input from files.
- **Environment Variables**: Environment variables are dynamic values that affect the behavior of processes. Common variables include PATH, HOME, and USER.
- **Runlevels (Targets in systemd)**: Runlevels are modes that define the state of the machine, such as whether it's in multi-user mode, single-user mode, or has a graphical interface. In systemd, these are referred to as targets.
- **Virtual Memory**: Virtual memory allows the system to use more memory than physically available by using disk space as a temporary extension of RAM.
- **File Descriptors**: File descriptors are references to open files or input/output resources. Standard file descriptors include stdin (0), stdout (1), and stderr (2).
- **Cron Jobs**: Cron jobs are scheduled tasks that run automatically at specified intervals. They are defined in the crontab file and are used for regular maintenance tasks.

- **Logging**: Linux keeps extensive logs of system activity in files like **/var/log/syslog** or **/var/log/messages**, which are critical for troubleshooting.
- **User and Group Management**: Linux manages users and groups to control access to system resources. Commands like useradd, usermod, and groupadd are used for this purpose.
- **Inodes**: Inodes are data structures that store information about files, such as permissions, ownership, and file type, but not the file name or content.
- **Filesystem Types**: Linux supports various filesystem types, including ext4, xfs, btrfs, ntfs, and vfat, each with its own features and use cases.
- **Process Signals**: Signals are software interrupts used to manage processes. Common signals include SIGINT (interrupt), SIGTERM (terminate), and SIGHUP (hang up).

Get details about your system

Getting information about a system and recording it correctly is important for a wide range of use cases. This allows one to recreate the same system environment and hence, work in same flow and get same performance measurements.

This involves both hardware and software details.

While working in a professional setting, often, one is required to keep a track of System details for every measurement/ experiment done. This is because at a later point the same performance can be replicated by creating same environment.

This is how a basic record of our system configuration looks like:

System Information	
Attribute	**Value**
Model	Intel(R) Xeon(R) Platinum 8180 CPU @ 2.50GHz
NUMA nodes	4
Sockets	2
Cores	28
Threads per socket	2
CPUs	112
Hyperthreading	OFF
Frequency	2494.256 MHz
RAM	512 GB
Rank	2

Attribute	Value
DIMMs	4
Clock Frequency	4200 MHz
Clock Speed	2133 MT/s
Software Information	
Attribute	**Value**
Kernel	Linux linux-mzys 4.4.162-94.72-default
GCC version	GCC (SUSE Linux) 6.2.1 20160826
OS	OpenSUSE 12.3 (Dartmouth)

We will go through the process so that you can recreate the details for your own system.

It is highly suggested that you try the commands in your system

---

We will get started with the process.

lscpu command

lscpu command will provide information about the CPU architecture by reading two files:

- sysfs
- /proc/cpuinfo

The output is the first step of collecting system configuration information. This command provides some key information which is used to run processes efficiently. The idea is that there are commands to control the execution of processes and we have explored this later in this book.

Command:

```
lscpu
```

We will present the output in our system first so that you can go through it and analyze it. We explain the background knowledge and go through the command following this.

It provides several information, so it is highly advised that you examine it carefully on your own first.

```
Architecture:          x86_64
CPU op-mode(s):        32-bit, 64-bit
Byte Order:            Little Endian
CPU(s):                112
On-line CPU(s) list:   0-111
Thread(s) per core:    2
Core(s) per socket:    28
Socket(s):             2
NUMA node(s):          4
Vendor ID:             GenuineIntel
CPU family:            6
Model:                 85
```

```
Model name:              Intel(R) Xeon(R) Platinum 8180 CPU @
2.50GHz
Stepping:                4
CPU MHz:                 2494.256
BogoMIPS:                4988.51
Virtualization:          VT-x
L1d cache:               32K
L1i cache:               32K
L2 cache:                1024K
L3 cache:                39424K
NUMA node0 CPU(s):
0,4,8,12,16,20,24,28,32,36,40,44,48,52,56,60,64,68,72,76,80,
84,88,92,96,100,104,108
NUMA node1 CPU(s):
1,5,9,13,17,21,25,29,33,37,41,45,49,53,57,61,65,69,73,77,81,
85,89,93,97,101,105,109
NUMA node2 CPU(s):
2,6,10,14,18,22,26,30,34,38,42,46,50,54,58,62,66,70,74,78,82
,86,90,94,98,102,106,110
NUMA node3 CPU(s):
3,7,11,15,19,23,27,31,35,39,43,47,51,55,59,63,67,71,75,79,83
,87,91,95,99,103,107,111
Flags:                   fpu vme de pse tsc msr pae mce cx8
apic sep mtrr pge mca cmov pat pse36 clflush dts acpi mmx
fxsr sse sse2 ss ht tm pbe syscall nx pdpe1gb rdtscp lm
constant_tsc art arch_perfmon pebs bts rep_good nopl
xtopology nonstop_tsc aperfmperf eagerfpu pni pclmulqdq
dtes64 monitor ds_cpl vmx smx est tm2 ssse3 sdbg fma cx16
xtpr pdcm pcid dca sse4_1 sse4_2 x2apic movbe popcnt
tsc_deadline_timer aes xsave avx f16c rdrand lahf_lm abm
3dnowprefetch ida arat epb invpcid_single pln pts dtherm
intel_pt kaiser tpr_shadow vnmi flexpriority ept vpid
fsgsbase tsc_adjust bmi1 hle avx2 smep bmi2 erms invpcid rtm
cqm mpx avx512f avx512dq rdseed adx smap clflushopt clwb
```

```
avx512cd avx512bw avx512vl xsaveopt xsavec xgetbv1 cqm_llc
cqm_occup_llc pku ospke
```

A system has a couple of NUMA nodes which is a division of the entire system. The idea is that processes can run on separate NUMA nodes without any interference and overhead for memory access point of view.

Each NUMA node has a set of CPUs and separate memory assigned to it.

In our case, with the lscpu command, we get the following information:

- We have 4 NUMA nodes
- We have 112 CPUs
- We get the entire list of CPUs and the NUMA node each belongs to.

We have sockets which are the number of distinct physical components. Each socket has a set of cores assigned to it.

Each core can have several CPUs assigned to it and the number of CPUs is same as the number of threads assigned to a core.

Note: A CPU can run only one thread at a time. A thread means one line of execution/ one process.

From our lscpu output, we get the following details:

- 2 sockets
- 28 cores per socket
- 2 threads per cores

If you do the calculation, the numbers will match on your system.

(Number of Sockets) x (Number of cores per socket) x (Number of threads per core) = (Number of CPUs)

2 x 28 x 2 = 112

Note: If hyperthreading (a property) is on, then the above calculation will not hold, and we will get the twice the number of CPUs. In hyperthreading, the number of threads per core is doubled. Hence, this gives us another key information: *the state of hyperthreading*.

If hyperthreading is on, then:

(Number of Sockets) x (Number of cores per socket) x (Number of threads per core) = (Number of CPUs) x 2

2 x 28 x 4 = 112 x 2

With this, we got a good idea of the system design. This information shall be recorded and will be used extensively in our later sections where we run processes efficiently.

We get other important details to identify our system as well. These are:

- Model name: Intel(R) Xeon(R) Platinum 8180 CPU @ 2.50GHz

CPU frequency is 2494.256 MHz. This is important as it impact performance of programs directly and must be same to enable us to replicate a benchmark result.

The flag values indicate the different features supported by the system. For example, AVX2 and AVX512 are supported in our system. For common systems, AVX512 is not supported and the performance of specific applications may be low which use AVX512 to their benefit.

This gives a good indication why the performance of the same application may vary significantly across systems.

Following is the summary of the key information we recorded using lscpu command:

System Information (lscpu)	
Attribute	Value
Model	Intel(R) Xeon(R) Platinum 8180 CPU @ 2.50GHz
NUMA nodes	4
Sockets	2
Cores	28

Threads per socket	2
CPUs	112
Hyperthreading	OFF
Frequency	2494.256 MHz

You must take a note of these details for your system as well. Do this before moving on to the next command.

uname -a

This command will provide the kernel name. This is important so because operating systems play a major role.

In most benchmarking setting, measurements are taken on different operating systems and hence, kernel is a key information.

Command:

```
uname -a
```

Sample output:

```
Linux linux-mzys 4.4.162-94.72-default #1
SMP Mon Nov 12 18:57:45 UTC 2018 (9de753f)
x86_64 x86_64 x86_64 GNU/Linux
```

Following is the record of our kernel information:

System Information (uname -a)	
Attribute	Value
Kernel	Linux linux-mzys 4.4.162-94.72-default

sudo dmidecode

This command provides several important information such as Desktop Management Interface and is linked to System Management BIOS. It provides the memory structure, system components, device information and much more.

We will investigate parts of it one by one to understand and get relevant information quickly.

Clock speed

The first information we need is the clock speed. We can grep MT on the output of sudo dmidecode to get this information conveniently. Grep is a UNIX tool which allows us to filter text.

```
sudo dmidecode | grep MT
```

Output:

```
MTRR (Memory type range registers)
        Speed: 2133 MT/s
        Configured Clock Speed: 1067 MT/s
```

In this command, we will get the Physical memory slot using grep DDR

```
sudo dmidecode | grep DDR
```

Output:

```
Type: DDR4
```

To get the memory rank, grep Rank as follows:

```
sudo dmidecode | grep Rank
```

Output:

```
Rank: 2
```

To get the clock frequency, use the following command:

```
sudo dmidecode | grep MHz
```

Output:

```
External Clock: 100 MHz
Max Speed: 4200 MHz
Current Speed: 3400 MHz
```

To get the DIMM information, get the following command:

```
sudo dmidecode | grep DIMM
```

Output:

```
Form Factor: DIMM
Locator: DIMM 0
Form Factor: DIMM
Locator: DIMM 1
```

To get the system memory/ RAM:

```
sudo dmidecode | grep GB
```

Output:

```
Maximum Capacity: 512 GB
Range Size: 128 GB
Range Size: 128 GB
Range Size: 128 GB
Range Size: 128 GB
```

Hence, our system has 512GB of RAM (Random Access Memory).

With this, following are the key information of our system which shall be recorded for all purposes:

System Information (dmidecode)	
Attribute	**Value**
RAM	512 GB
Rank	2
DIMMs	4
Clock Frequency	4200 MHz
Clock Speed	2133 MT/s

Other **dmidecode** commands you should try out are:

- sudo dmidecode -s system-manufacturer
- sudo dmidecode | grep Product
- sudo dmidecode -s system-product-name
- sudo dmidecode | egrep -i 'manufacturer|product'
- sudo dmidecode | egrep -i 'vendor'

These commands provide important information involving the manufacturer/ vendor of your system and much more.

A computing system has several key components like processor, motherboard and more. These are the dmidecode commands to get information regarding these components:

- sudo dmidecode -t processor (for the processor)
- sudo dmidecode -t system

- sudo dmidecode -t baseboard
- sudo dmidecode -t chassis
- sudo dmidecode -t bios
- sudo dmidecode -t cache

You must try the above commands on your system, record the output and analyze it carefully.

cat /proc/meminfo

meminfo is a file in Linux system that stores the information related to memory usage. To get memory statistics of your system, use this command:

```
cat /proc/meminfo
```

Output:

```
MemTotal:       394877600 kB
MemFree:        322057928 kB
MemAvailable:   391704744 kB
Buffers:          2735168 kB
Cached:          66592340 kB
SwapCached:         39408 kB
Active:          44374924 kB
```

```
Inactive:          25087292 kB
Active(anon):         89332 kB
Inactive(anon):       94996 kB
Active(file):      44285592 kB
Inactive(file):    24992296 kB
Unevictable:             80 kB
Mlocked:                 80 kB
SwapTotal:         16779260 kB
SwapFree:          12971548 kB
Dirty:                    0 kB
Writeback:                4 kB
AnonPages:            98584 kB
Mapped:               73280 kB
Shmem:                49620 kB
Slab:               2853688 kB
SReclaimable:       2744528 kB
SUnreclaim:          109160 kB
KernelStack:          20608 kB
PageTables:            7668 kB
NFS_Unstable:             0 kB
Bounce:                   0 kB
WritebackTmp:             0 kB
CommitLimit:      214218060 kB
Committed_AS:       4248960 kB
VmallocTotal:    34359738367 kB
VmallocUsed:              0 kB
VmallocChunk:             0 kB
HardwareCorrupted:        0 kB
AnonHugePages:        32768 kB
HugePages_Total:          0
HugePages_Free:           0
HugePages_Rsvd:           0
HugePages_Surp:           0
Hugepagesize:          2048 kB
DirectMap4k:         669504 kB
DirectMap2M:       50388992 kB
```

```
DirectMap1G:      352321536 kB
```

This gives good insights and you must analyze it carefully.

gcc –version

This command is used to get the gcc version. This is an important information to record as gcc plays a major role in a wide range of applications.

Depending on the application/ focus on hand, we need to track different information.

Command:

```
gcc --version
```

Output:

```
gcc (SUSE Linux) 6.2.1 20160826 [gcc-6-branch revision 239773]
Copyright (C) 2016 Free Software Foundation, Inc.
This is free software; see the source for copying conditions.  There is NO
warranty; not even for MERCHANTABILITY or FITNESS FOR A PARTICULAR PURPOSE.
```

So, the GCC detected is: GCC (SUSE Linux) 6.2.1 20160826

lsb_release -a

This command is used to get details of the operating system.

Command:

```
lsb_release -a
```

Output:

```
LSB Version:    n/a
Distributor ID: SUSE
Description:     openSUSE 12.3 (Dartmouth) (x86_64)
Release:         12.3
Codename:        n/a
```

With this, we get the operating system as OpenSUSE 12.3 (Dartmouth).

With this, we get two key information which is recorded as:

Software Information	
Attribute	**Value**

GCC version	GCC (SUSE Linux) 6.2.1 20160826
OS	OpenSUSE 12.3 (Dartmouth)

The entire sample record of System and Software details for our computing system is as follows:

System Information	
Attribute	**Value**
Model	Intel(R) Xeon(R) Platinum 8180 CPU @ 2.50GHz
NUMA nodes	4
Sockets	2
Cores	28
Threads per socket	2
CPUs	112
Hyperthreading	OFF
Frequency	2494.256 MHz
RAM	512 GB
Rank	2
DIMMs	4
Clock Frequency	4200 MHz
Clock Speed	2133 MT/s
Software Information	
Attribute	**Value**
Kernel	Linux linux-mzys 4.4.162-94.72-default
GCC version	GCC (SUSE Linux) 6.2.1 20160826
OS	OpenSUSE 12.3 (Dartmouth)

You should follow the commands, run it on your system and make your own table of system and software information. This is important as you shall prepare this everything you run a software on a particular system so that other professional programmers can replicate your work.

Fill this table for your system:

System Information	
Attribute	**Value**
Model	
NUMA nodes	
Sockets	
Cores	
Threads per socket	
CPUs	
Hyperthreading	
Frequency	
RAM	
Rank	
DIMMs	
Clock Frequency	
Clock Speed	
Software Information	
Attribute	**Value**
Kernel	
GCC version	
OS	

With this, we will move on to work with processes that is running commands/ applications on our systems.

Run a process in background

Running a process in the background means that the process will not occupy the screen and we can continue working on it with different commands. The process will continue running but output can come to the screen but it will not take any input. We can later bring it back on the screen as well.

In short, the syntax is:

```
<command> &
```

Note that this does not mean that the process will continue to run on closing the terminal.

Note, there are two types of processes namely:

- background process
- foreground process

The idea is that the background process does not link with the STDOUT and STDERR pipes of the screen session while foreground process is linked with the STDOUT and STDERR pipes of the screen session. Hence, if the background process produces an output in the terminal, it will get printed. So, it is useful if a process does not produce any output or output is piped to a file.

Note that both background and foreground processes are linked with STDIN pipe. So, if a background process needs an input from STDIN pipe, it gets stuck (hang) until we bring it to the foreground.

To make a process run in the background, we need to append the command with &.

Syntax:

```
command &
```

Example:

```
python code.py &
```

It will give an output as:

```
[1] 121378
```

1 is the job id and 121378 is the process id.

Check background processes

We can check the processes that are in background as follows:

```
jobs
```

The output in our case is as follows:

```
[1]-  Running          python code.py &
[2]+  Running          python opengenus.py &
```

The first integer is the Job ID of the command that is given along side.

For example, the command "**python opengenus.py &**" has Job ID 2. We can use the Job ID to manage the background process and do several things like:

- bring a background process to foreground
- killing a background process

Bring a process back

To bring a process back in foreground, we need to use the following command:

```
fg %<job_ib>
```

Example:

```
fg %2
```

This will bring the process "python opengenus.py &" to the foreground. The output will be like:

```
(base) [opengenus@localhost Desktop]$ fg %2
python opengenus.py
```

If your code is waiting for an input, it can be provided now.

Make a running process go into background

Now, if your process is already running and you want to take it to the background, you can follow the following steps:

```
Press control key + Z

// check job id using jobs
jobs

// make job go to background
bg %<job id>
```

The process will have moved to the background.

If you just press control key + z. It will stop the process which we can see in the jobs command:

```
[1]  Running          python code.py &
[2]- Running          python opengenus.py &
[3]+ Stopped          python code_2.py
```

Now, if we move the Job ID 3 to background using bg command, we can check the impact using the jobs command.

```
bg %3
```

It will give an output as:

```
[3]+ python code_2.py &
```

Note the & sign at the end. It signifies that the process is running in the background.

Try the jobs command:

```
jobs
```

The output will be as follows:

```
[1]  Running          python code.py &
[2]- Running          python opengenus.py &
[3]+ Running           python code_2.py &
```

Get Process ID of a job

We can get the process ID of all background jobs using the jobs command as follows:

```
jobs -l
```

The output will be as follows:

```
[1]  121378 Running          python code.py &
[2]- 127536 Running          python opengenus.py &
[3]+ 12623 Running           python code_2.py &
```

Note that the first number (1, 2 and 3) are Job IDs while the second numbers (like 121378) are Process ID.

Kill a process

There are two ways to kill a process:

- Kill it directly using process ID
- Bring it to foreground and kill it using control + C

  Once we get the process ID of a job, we can kill it directly like:

```
kill 121378
```

This will kill the first job. It will give an output as:

```
[1]   Terminated          python code.py
```

We can verify this using our jobs command as follows:

```
jobs -l
```

The output will be as:

```
[2]- 127536 Running           python opengenus.py &
[3]+ 12623 Running            python code_2.py &
```

Notice that the first background job is missing.

We will use the second approach of bring it to the foreground and killing it as follows.

```
fg %3
```

This will give an output as:

```
(base) [opengenus@localhost Desktop]$ fg %3
python code_2.py
```

The terminal is stuck. If we press Control + C, the process will be terminated as follows:

```
(base) [opengenus@localhost Desktop]$ fg %3
python code_2.py
^CTraceback (most recent call last):
  File "code.py", line 7, in <module>
    time.sleep(1)
KeyboardInterrupt
```

We can verify this using **jobs -l** command.

```
jobs -l
```

The output will be as follows:

```
[2]+ 127536 Running              python opengenus.py &
```

Hence, only process is in the background.

With this, you have the complete knowledge of working with background process.

The problem with this is that if you close the terminal it will kill the process. To enable the process to continue even after closing the terminal, we need to detach the process from the terminal which can be done using screen, disown and nohup.

Screen command

Screen is an application in Linux system which is used to manage terminal sessions and run processes even when the terminal screen is closed. In this guide, we have demonstrated all screen commands so that you can use it in your daily work.

The most common use of screen command is **running processes in background**.

Install Screen

We can install screen application on Linux versions like Ubuntu as follows:

```
sudo apt-get install screen
```

For other systems like RedHat (RHEL), we can use:

```
sudo yum install screen
```

Start a screen session

To start a screen session, use the following command:

```
screen
```

This will open a new session with a clear screen. We can work on this screen and use the features provided by screen application for it.

Get help of screen

To get the help options of screen application, press the following keys in order:

```
Control key + A key  followed by ? key
```

Note: for this to work, you should be within a screen session.

Following is the output:

```
          Screen key bindings, page 1 of 2.

          Command key: ^A   Literal ^A: a

break     ^B b      license   ,         removebuf  =
clear     C         lockscreen ^X x     reset    Z
colon     :         log       H         screen    ^C c
copy      ^[ [      login     L         select    '
detach    ^D d      meta      a         silence   _
digraph   ^V        monitor   M         split    S
displays  *         next      ^@ ^N sp n  suspend   ^Z z
```

```
dumptermcap .       number   N       time      ^T t
fit      F       only    Q       title     A
flow     ^F f    other   ^A      vbell     ^G
focus    ^I      pow_break B       version   v
hardcopy h       pow_detach D      width     W
help     ?       prev    ^H ^P p ^? windows  ^W w
history  { }     quit    \       wrap      ^R r
info     i       readbuf <       writebuf  >
kill     K k     redisplay ^L l   xoff      ^S s
lastmsg  ^M m    remove  X       xon       ^Q q


            [Press Space for next page; Return to end.]
```

Exit a screen session

To exit a screen session, we can detach it using the following keys:

```
Control key + A followed by d
```

The output will be like:

```
[detached from 129921.pts-1.localhost]
(base) [opengenus@localhost ~]$
```

129921.pts-1.localhost is the name of our screen session and we can use this name to get back into it.

This will allow us to get back into this screen session later and the processes within it will keep running on the system. We will see later in section "Delete a screen session" to learn how we can delete it and terminate all processes within it.

List existing screen sessions

Once we are out of a screen session, we may go back into it. For this, we shall use the following command:

```
screen -ls
```

In our case, following is the output:

```
There are screens on:
    129921.pts-1.localhost  (Detached)
    120455.pts-1.localhost  (Detached)
2 Sockets in /var/run/screen/S-opengenus.
```

We have two screen sessions namely:

129921
120455

We can go back into one of the sessions as well.

Run a command in a screen session

The advantage of using screen is that you can run a command in a screen session and then, close the terminal and even then, the process will continue to run. It is useful if you are working on a remote machine or need to close the terminal.

The flow will be as follows:

```
// create a screen session
screen

// run the command now in background
command &

// exit the screen
control key + A followed by d

// now you can close the terminal safely
exit
```

Go back into a session

To go back into an existing screen session, we should get the name of the session (say 129921) using the list screen command and use the following command:

```
screen -r 129921
```

This will give you access to the session.

How to know you are in a screen?

The simplest way to detect is to do the screen list command and if any screen session is active, it may signify that you or some other user is within it.

```
screen -ls
```

Alternatively, you can try to exit a screen as well. If you within a screen, it will get detacted and if you are not in one, it will not work.

```
control key + A followed by d
```

Delete a screen session

To delete a screen session, we need to get into the screen session we want to delete and following it, there are two options:

Use exit command as:

```
exit
```

Use the following command:

```
Control key + A followed by k
```

A prompt will come as:

```
Really kill this window [y/n]
```

On pressing y key, the screen session is terminated with the following message:

```
[screen is terminating]
(base) [opengenus@localhost ~]$
```

This will terminate the session and kill all process within it.

Name a screen session

We may need to name a screen session so that when we list the sessions, we can understand which session is for which task.

To do this, during the creation of a screen session, we can use the following command:

```
screen -S name
```

This will create a screen session named "name" and following is the output of the screen list command:

```
There are screens on:
    113050.name    (Detached)
    105349.pts-1.localhost  (Detached)
    129921.pts-1.localhost  (Detached)
    120455.pts-1.localhost  (Detached)
4 Sockets in /var/run/screen/S-opengenus.
```

Lock your screen session

If you want to lock your screen session, you can use the following key combination:

```
control key + A followed by x
```

This will turn the screen into this:

```
Screen used by opengenus <opengenus> on localhost.
Password:
```

One can enter the UNIX user password to log back into the session.

Log screen session activity

We can log all activity in a screen session by creating a session using the following command:

```
screen -L
```

If one is already in a screen session, one can use the following key combination:

```
control key + A followed by H
```

This will save a file with all activity.

There are several other options available with screen application. You may go through the help option that we have demonstrate previously and try out each option. In fact, the options we have demonstrate are enough to use screen like a master.

File handling

We have created the folder structure with files as a workspace to work on.

```
--- file1
--- folder1.0.0
--- --- --- file2
--- --- --- folder1.1.0
--- --- --- --- --- --- folder1.1.1
--- --- --- --- --- --- file3
--- --- --- --- --- --- file4
--- --- --- folder1.2.0
--- folder2.0.0
--- --- --- file5
```

We will work on this.

ls command is used to list the files and directories in the current directory level.

Command:

```
ls
```

Output:

```
file1  folder1.0.0  folder2.0.0
```

"ls -l" command is an incremental to the above "ls" command where other key information are included like size of file/ directory, modified date, owner, permissions and much more.

Command:

```
ls -l
```

Output:

```
total 0
-rw-rw-r--. 1 opengenus aditya  0 Aug  7 00:10 file1
drwxrwxr-x. 4 opengenus aditya 57 Aug  7 00:11 folder1.0.0
drwxrwxr-x. 2 opengenus aditya 19 Aug  7 00:11 folder2.0.0
```

"ls -R"

This is an important command as it lists out all files and sub-directories recursively to any depth.

Command:

```
ls -R
```

Output:

```
.:
file1  folder1.0.0  folder2.0.0

./folder1.0.0:
file2  folder1.1.0  folder1.2.0

./folder1.0.0/folder1.1.0:
folder1.1.1

./folder1.0.0/folder1.1.0/folder1.1.1:
file3  file4

./folder1.0.0/folder1.2.0:

./folder2.0.0:
file5
```

Other ls commands you should try quickly are:

- **ls -n** (to display user ID and group ID of files and directories)
- **ls relative_or_absolute_path** (ls on specific directory and not on current working directory)
- **ls -i** (to get inode numbers)
- **ls -lS** (to get files in order of file size)

- **ls -F** (to add / after every directory)
- **ls -lh** (to display size in human readable format)
- **ls –help** (to display the guide on using ls)

top/ htop command

While running an application, we may need to monitor how the system is being used. This can be done using the top or htop command.

Top command comes by default.

Command:

```
top
```

Output:

```
top - 02:35:41 up 27 days,  9:00,  1 user,  load average: 0.00, 0.00, 0.00
Tasks: 2215 total,   1 running, 2214 sleeping,   0 stopped,   0 zombie
%Cpu(s):  0.0 us,  0.0 sy,  0.0 ni,100.0 id,  0.0 wa,  0.0 hi,  0.0 si,  0.0 st
MiB Mem : 1031518.+total, 1007743.+free,   3076.1 used,  20698.8 buff/cache
MiB Swap:   4096.0 total,   4096.0 free,      0.0 used. 1023293.+avail Mem

    PID USER      PR  NI    VIRT    RES    SHR S  %CPU  %MEM     TIME+ COMMAND
 483516 root      20   0   66996   7312   4020 R   1.6   0.0   0:00.43 top
   5541 root      20   0       0      0      0 I   0.3   0.0  13:04.38 kworker/158:3-events
      1 root      20   0  245492  14460   9300 S   0.0   0.0   0:17.81 systemd
      2 root      20   0       0      0      0 S   0.0   0.0   0:01.09 kthreadd
      3 root       0 -20       0      0      0 I   0.0   0.0   0:00.00 rcu_gp
      4 root       0 -20       0      0      0 I   0.0   0.0   0:00.00 rcu_par_gp
      6 root       0 -20       0      0      0 I   0.0   0.0   0:00.00 kworker/0:0H-kblockd
      7 root      20   0       0      0      0 I   0.0   0.0   0:00.65 kworker/u512:0-netns
      9 root       0 -20       0      0      0 I   0.0   0.0   0:00.00 mm_percpu_wq
     10 root      20   0       0      0      0 S   0.0   0.0   0:00.21 ksoftirqd/0
     11 root      20   0       0      0      0 I   0.0   0.0  27:08.99 rcu_sched
     12 root      rt   0       0      0      0 S   0.0   0.0   0:00.05 migration/0
     13 root      rt   0       0      0      0 S   0.0   0.0   0:00.69 watchdog/0
     14 root      20   0       0      0      0 S   0.0   0.0   0:00.00 cpuhp/0
     15 root      20   0       0      0      0 S   0.0   0.0   0:00.00 cpuhp/1
     16 root      rt   0       0      0      0 S   0.0   0.0   0:01.56 watchdog/1
     17 root      rt   0       0      0      0 S   0.0   0.0   0:00.01 migration/1
     18 root      20   0       0      0      0 S   0.0   0.0   0:00.09 ksoftirqd/1
     20 root       0 -20       0      0      0 I   0.0   0.0   0:00.00 kworker/1:0H-events_highpri
     21 root      20   0       0      0      0 S   0.0   0.0   0:00.00 cpuhp/2
     22 root      rt   0       0      0      0 S   0.0   0.0   0:01.53 watchdog/2
     23 root      rt   0       0      0      0 S   0.0   0.0   0:00.01 migration/2
     24 root      20   0       0      0      0 S   0.0   0.0   0:00.05 ksoftirqd/2
     26 root       0 -20       0      0      0 I   0.0   0.0   0:00.00 kworker/2:0H-events_highpri
     27 root      20   0       0      0      0 S   0.0   0.0   0:00.00 cpuhp/3
     28 root      rt   0       0      0      0 S   0.0   0.0   0:01.63 watchdog/3
     29 root      rt   0       0      0      0 S   0.0   0.0   0:00.01 migration/3
```

To install htop, you may use the command:

```
sudo apt-get install htop
```

htop is an improvement over top and should be used preferably. It displays the thread utilization visually.

Command:

```
htop
```

Output:

It is, highly advised in a professional development setting that you run htop on one terminal while running an application and observe the utilization in htop output.

vi command

To open a file, you can use the vi command simply.

Command:

```
vi filename
```

This will open a terminal where the file contents will be displayed. To start writing, press "I" key and you will go to insert mode.

To go to command mode, press ESC key and then use the following commands (without quotes and followed by enter):

- ":q" -> quit vi editor
- ":q!" -> quit vi editor without saving unsaved changes
- ":w" -> save unsaved changes
- ":wq" -> save unsaved changes and quit editor
- ":<integer>" -> go to line number as the specified integer
- :/<text> -> to find the particular text

Other related commands you must explore are:

- pwd (displays the absolute path of present working directory)
- du (lists out directories with memory occupied)
- du -mh (same as above command + get size in MB)

- cat filename (to get file contents in terminal)

There are several other commands, but these commands will give you a good understanding and enable you to start you work smoothly without any friction.

CONCLUDING NOTE

Key advices:

- Always keep track of system details
- Version of software components play a major role and can be source of bugs. Keep track of it.
- Always ensure no process is running in background before running a new command (to ensure performance is not impacted)
- Always analyze htop output while a command is running
- Always run process that will consume time as a background process (to save time)

With practice and as situation arises, you will be able to master using Linux.

Best of luck for your upcoming job/ interview.

With the current Linux knowledge, you will be able to work in a professional development setting smoothly and make huge contributions from the first day.